Pre-Algebra Basics

Glenview, Illinois
Needham, Massachusetts
Upper Saddle River, New Jersey

Staff Credits

Barbara Albright, Janet Fauser, Brian Kane, Marie Mathis, Sandra Morris, Cindy Noftle, Angie Seltzer, David B. Spangler, Jeff Weidenaar

Additional Credits

Steve Curtis Design, Inc., Barbara Hardt, Anne S. Ryan, Stet Graphics, Inc., Ziebka Editorial Services

© Prentice-Hall, Inc.

Prentice Hall

Pre-Algebra Basics

Table of Contents

SKILL 2: Absolute Value

The **absolute value** of a number is its distance from 0 on the number line.

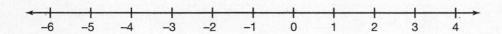

The symbol for absolute value is $|\ \ |$. Since −5 is 5 units from 0, the absolute value of −5 is 5. In symbols, $|-5| = 5$. The distance from 0 to 3 is 3 units, so $|3| = 3$.

An integer and its opposite are the same distance from 0 on the number line. This means that a number and its opposite always have the same absolute value. For example, $|-5| = 5$ and $|5| = 5$.

Example 1

Find $|-2|$.

On the number line, −2 is 2 units from 0. So $|-2| = 2$.

Example 2

Name the two integers that have an absolute value of 8.

Start at 0 on the number line and count 8 units to the left. You arrive at −8, so $|-8| = 8$.

Start at 0 on the number line and count 8 units to the right. You arrive at 8, so $|8| = 8$.

The two integers with an absolute value of 8 are −8 and 8.

Guided Practice

Find each absolute value. Refer to the number line if you need help.

1. $|-7|$

   −7 is _____ units from 0.

   So $|-7| =$ _____.

2. $|6|$

   6 is _____ units from 0.

   So $|6| =$ _____.

Use a number line to complete the sentences.

3. Start at 0 and go 4 units to the left. You arrive at _____. So $|-4| =$ _____.

4. Start at 0 and go 4 units to the right. You arrive at _____. So $|4| =$ _____.

5. The two integers with an absolute value of 4 are _____ and _____.

SKILL 2: Practice

Find each absolute value.

1. $|10| = $ _____
2. $|-29| = $ _____
3. $|-13| = $ _____

4. $|92| = $ _____
5. $|36| = $ _____
6. $|-56| = $ _____

7. $|0| = $ _____
8. $|80| = $ _____
9. $|-400| = $ _____

10. $|21| = $ _____
11. $|-48| = $ _____
12. $|-47| = $ _____

13. $|42| = $ _____
14. $|-31| = $ _____
15. $|74| = $ _____

16. $|17| = $ _____
17. $|-17| = $ _____
18. $|-74| = $ _____

Name two integers that have the given absolute value.

19. 14 _____
20. 3 _____

21. 32 _____
22. 19 _____

23. 20 _____
24. 100 _____

25. 45 _____
26. 53 _____

27. 96 _____
28. 400 _____

29. 84 _____
30. 37 _____

Solve.

31. Elevations above sea level are represented
by positive numbers. Elevations below sea level
are represented by negative numbers. What
two elevations have an absolute value of 1,000 ft? _____

32. Find $|-11|$.

Skill 2

A -11 C 1
B -1 D 11

33. What is the opposite of -36?

Skill 1

F 63   H 0
G 36   J -63

SKILL 3: Comparing and Ordering Integers

You can use the number line to help compare two integers.
Integers become greater as you move to the right.

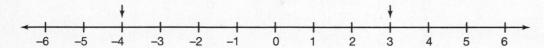

On the number line above, 3 is to the right of -4, so 3 is greater than -4. The symbols $>$, $<$, and $=$ are used to compare integers. Since 3 is greater than -4, you can write $3 > -4$, or $-4 < 3$.

To order a set of integers from least to greatest, locate them on the number line. Then list them in order from left to right.

Example 1

Use $>$, $<$, or $=$ to compare the numbers.

a. $-1 \bigcirc -5$

-1 is to the right of -5.

So $-1 > -5$.

b. $-6 \bigcirc -2$

-6 is to the left of -2.

So $-6 < -2$.

Example 2

Order the integers 2, -3, 5, and -1 from least to greatest.

Locate the integers on the number line.

List the integers from left to right. From least to greatest the integers are -3, -1, 2, and 5.

Guided Practice

Use $>$, $<$, or $=$ to compare the numbers. Refer to the number line.

1. $-6 \bigcirc -1$

2. $5 \bigcirc -5$

3. $|-4| \bigcirc 2$

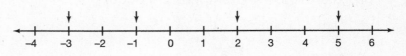

4. List the integers -3, -6, and 4 from least to greatest. _____

SKILL 3: Practice

Use >, <, or = to compare the numbers.

1. −6 ◯ −5
2. 1 ◯ −4
3. 12 ◯ −20

4. 9 ◯ 15
5. −8 ◯ −12
6. −30 ◯ 0

7. −20 ◯ 13
8. −16 ◯ 16
9. 18 ◯ |−18|

10. 40 ◯ −100
11. −50 ◯ 45
12. 6 ◯ −36

13. 0 ◯ −32
14. |7| ◯ 7
15. |−3| ◯ |−8|

16. |17| ◯ 17
17. |−17| ◯ 17
18. −74 ◯ 60

Order each set of integers from least to greatest.

19. −9, 4, 0

_____

20. −7, −8, −4

_____

21. −3, 2, 6, −10

_____

22. 10, −20, 30, −30

_____

23. −5, 17, −19, 6

_____

24. 3, −3, 10, −10

_____

Solve.

25. The low temperature on Monday was 5°F, the low temperature on Tuesday was −5°F, and the low temperature on Wednesday was −1°F. On which day did the lowest temperature occur? _____

26. Which list shows the integers −3, −4, and 2 in order from least to greatest?

    Skill 3

    A −4, −3, 2   C 2, −3, −4
    B −3, −4, 2   D 2, −4, −3

27. Find |28|.

    Skill 2

    F −28   H 28
    G 0   J 56

SKILL 4: Addition of Integers

You can think of adding integers as making moves on a number line.

Example 1

a. Use the number line to find 2 + 3.

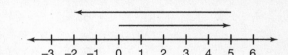

Start at 0. Move 2 units to the right.
Then move 3 more units to the right.
So, 2 + 3 = 5.

b. Use the number line to find 5 + (−7).

Start at 0. Move 5 units to the right.
Then move 7 units to the left.
So, 5 + (−7) = −2.

You can also add integers without the number line.

To add two integers with the same sign: Add the absolute values of the numbers. The sum has the same sign as the addends.

To add integers with different signs: Find their absolute values. The sum is in the direction of the number with the larger absolute value. Subtract the smaller absolute value from the larger to find out how far the sum is in that direction.

Example 2

a. Find −4 + (−6).

$|-4| = 4$, and $|-6| = 6$.

Both numbers are negative.
Add the absolute values, 4 and 6,
to get 10. Use the negative sign.
So, −4 + (−6) = −10.

b. Find 7 + (−9).

$|-7| = 7$, and $|-9| = 9$.

The numbers have different signs.
Subtract the smaller absolute value, 7,
from 9 to obtain 2. The number −9
has a larger absolute value than the
number 7, so the answer is negative.
So, 7 + (−9) = −2.

Guided Practice

1. Use the number line to find −3 + 6.

Start at 0. Move _____ units to the left. Then

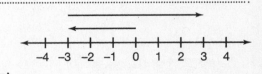

move _____ units to the right. So, −3 + 6 = _____.

2. Find −4 + 7.

The numbers have different signs. Subtract the smaller absolute value

from the larger to get _____. Since 7 has a larger absolute value than −4,

the sign of the answer is _____. So, −4 + 7 = _____.

SKILL 4: Practice

Use the number line to find each sum.

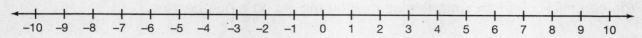

1. $-2 + 7 =$ _____
2. $3 + (-5) =$ _____
3. $5 + 3 =$ _____

4. $7 + (-8) =$ _____
5. $8 + (-8) =$ _____
6. $-3 + (-2) =$ _____

7. $-4 + 9 =$ _____
8. $2 + (-9) =$ _____
9. $3 + (-1) =$ _____

10. $-6 + (-2) =$ _____
11. $4 + 5 =$ _____
12. $-8 + 5 =$ _____

13. $7 + 3 =$ _____
14. $-3 + 2 =$ _____
15. $5 + (-4) =$ _____

Add the integers.

16. $-7 + 12 =$ _____
17. $35 + (-1) =$ _____
18. $-10 + (-12) =$ _____

19. $-6 + (-5) =$ _____
20. $0 + (-6) =$ _____
21. $50 + (-2) =$ _____

22. $1 + (-7) =$ _____
23. $15 + (-15) =$ _____
24. $2 + (-9) =$ _____

25. $-31 + 3 =$ _____
26. $4 + (-12) =$ _____
27. $-23 + 8 =$ _____

28. $10 + (-15) =$ _____
29. $42 + 16 =$ _____
30. $-1 + (-4) =$ _____

Solve.

31. The temperature in Middlefield at 6 A.M. was $-15°F$.
By 3 P.M., the temperature had risen $19°F$. What was
the temperature at 3 P.M.?   _____

32. A diver was 7 m below the surface of the water.
The diver then descended 3 m. What integer
represents the diver's position after the descent?   _____

33. Find $-12 + 8$.
Skill 4

   A -20 **C** 4

   B -4 **D** 20

34. Which number is less than -12?
Skill 3

   F -14 **H** -3

   G -11 **J** 4

SKILL 5: Subtraction of Integers

The number line at the right shows how you can
find the answer for the subtraction problem 3 − 5.
Start at 0 and go 3 units to the right. From 3, go
5 units to the left. You stop at −2. So, 3 − 5 = −2.

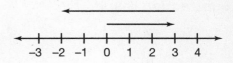

Notice that the addition problem 3 + (−5) also has the answer −2.
The second number in the addition problem is the opposite of the
number that was subtracted in the subtraction problem.

You can use this idea to subtract any two integers.

To subtract two integers: Add the opposite of the number being subtracted.

Change
subtraction to addition.

8 − 10   8 + (−10)

Add the opposite
of the number being subtracted.

The answer for 8 − 10 is the same as the answer for 8 + (−10). So, 8 − 10 = −2.

Example

Find −10 −7.

Change −10 −7 to the addition problem −10 + (−7).
Both the numbers in the addition problem are negative.
Add the absolute values to obtain 17, and use the negative sign.
So, −10 −7 = −17.

Guided Practice

**Write an addition for each subtraction. Then show the
subtraction result.**

1. 9 − 12

Addition: 9 + (−12) = _____

So, 9 − 12 = _____.

2. −5 − (−9)

Addition: −5 + 9 = _____

So, −5 − (−9) = _____.

3. 6 − (−7)

Addition: 6 + _____ = _____

So, 6 − (−7) = _____.

4. 2 − 11

Addition: 2 + (_____) = _____

So, 2 − 11 = _____.

SKILL 5: Practice

Write an addition for each subtraction. Then show the subtraction result.

1. 10 − 14

Addition: _____

So, 10 − 14 = _____.

2. −3 − 11

Addition: _____

So, −3 − 11 = _____.

3. −8 − (−6)

Addition: _____

So, −8 − (−6) = _____.

4. 50 − (−9)

Addition: _____

So, 50 − (−9) = _____.

5. −15 − 8

Addition: _____

So, −15 − 8 = _____.

6. 20 − 55

Addition: _____

So, 20 − 55 = _____.

Subtract.

7. −1 − (−15) _____

8. 20 − 3 _____

9. 11 − (−5) _____

10. 20 − 2 _____

11. −12 − (−12) _____

12. −2 − (−4) _____

13. 7 − 13 _____

14. 3 − 5 _____

15. −6 − 11 _____

16. 9 − 16 _____

17. 0 − (−7) _____

18. −4 − (−1) _____

19. 5 − (−3) _____

20. −9 − 25 _____

21. −18 − 10 _____

22. −11 − (−8) _____

23. −16 − 9 _____

24. 10 − (−9) _____

25. −25 − (−40) _____

26. −48 − 0 _____

27. −8 − 7 _____

Solve.

28. The elevation of New Orleans, Louisiana, is 8 feet below sea level. The elevation of Lake Champlain, Vermont, is 95 feet above sea level. How much higher is the elevation of Lake Champlain than New Orleans?

_____

29. In Fairbanks, Alaska, a typical January temperature is −13°F and a typical April temperature is 30°F. What is the difference between these temperatures?

_____

30. Find 2 − 9.   *Skill 5*

    A 11   **C** −7

    B 7   **D** −11

31. Find −2 + 8.   *Skill 4*

    F 10   **H** −6

    G 6   **J** −10

SKILL 6: Multiplication of Integers

Study the patterns below for multiplying integers.
(Note that the raised dot can be used instead of × to show multiplication.)

$3 \cdot 2 = 6$	$-4 \cdot 2 = -8$
$3 \cdot 1 = 3$	$-4 \cdot 1 = -4$
$3 \cdot 0 = 0$	$-4 \cdot 0 = 0$
$3 \cdot (-1) = -3$	$-4 \cdot (-1) = 4$
$3 \cdot (-2) = -6$	$-4 \cdot (-2) = 8$

Note that a positive integer multiplied by a positive integer is positive; a positive integer multiplied by a negative integer is negative.

Note that a negative integer multiplied by a positive integer is negative; a negative integer multiplied by a negative integer is positive.

The product of two numbers with the same sign is positive.
The product of two numbers with different signs is negative.
The product of 0 and any number is 0.

Example

Multiply.

a. $-3 \cdot (-6) = 18$ Both integers are negative, so the product is positive.

b. $-5 \cdot 7 = -35$ The integers have different signs, so the product is negative.

c. $8 \cdot (-4) = -32$ The integers have different signs, so the product is negative.

d. $0 \cdot (-9) = 0$ One of the integers is 0, so the product is zero.

Guided Practice

Tell whether the product is positive, negative, or 0. Then multiply.

1. $2 \cdot (7)$

The integers have the same sign.

The product is _____.

So, $2 \cdot (7) =$ _____.

2. $5 \cdot (-6)$

The integers have different signs.

The product is _____.

So, $5 \cdot (-6) =$ _____.

3. $-21 \cdot 0$

The second integer is 0.

The product is _____.

So, $-21 \cdot 0 =$ _____.

4. $(-10) \cdot (-7)$

The integers have the same sign.

The product is _____.

So, $(-10) \cdot (-7) =$ _____.

SKILL 6: Practice

Tell whether the product is positive, negative, or 0. Then multiply.

1. $-2 \cdot 10$

_____

$-2 \cdot 10 =$ _____

2. $-8 \cdot (-9)$

_____

$-8 \cdot (-9) =$ _____

3. $7 \cdot 15$

_____

$7 \cdot 15 =$ _____

4. $0 \cdot (-23)$

_____

$0 \cdot (-23) =$ _____

5. $-42 \cdot 3$

_____

$-42 \cdot 3 =$ _____

6. $-12 \cdot (-15)$

_____

$-12 \cdot (-15) =$ _____

Multiply.

7. $-2 \cdot 4 =$ _____

8. $-5 \cdot 6 =$ _____

9. $4 \cdot (-5) =$ _____

10. $-1 \cdot (-13) =$ _____

11. $2 \cdot (-8) =$ _____

12. $5 \cdot 19 =$ _____

13. $-3 \cdot (-6) =$ _____

14. $7 \cdot (-4) =$ _____

15. $-8 \cdot 11 =$ _____

16. $-6 \cdot 20 =$ _____

17. $-3 \cdot (-12) =$ _____

18. $-4 \cdot 5 =$ _____

19. $-7 \cdot 7 =$ _____

20. $6 \cdot (-10) =$ _____

21. $-8 \cdot (-15) =$ _____

22. $-20 \cdot (-5) =$ _____

23. $8 \cdot (-30) =$ _____

24. $-20 \cdot 20 =$ _____

25. $-7 \cdot (-13) =$ _____

26. $14 \cdot (-5) =$ _____

27. $25 \cdot 3 =$ _____

28. $9 \cdot (-30) =$ _____

29. $-20 \cdot (-30) =$ _____

30. $0 \cdot (-16) =$ _____

Solve.

31. There was a temperature change of $-2°F$ each hour over a period of 5 hours. In all, what was the temperature change over the 5-hour period?   _____

32. The price of a share of stock increased $3 each week over a 7-week period. What was the total change in the price of a share of the stock over this period of time?   _____

33. Find $-5 \cdot 3$.

Skill 6

A -15 **C** 2

B -2 **D** 15

34. Find $-8 + 20$.

Skill 4

F -28 **H** 12

G -12 **J** 28

SKILL 7: Division of Integers

In the previous lesson you learned the rules for deciding what sign to use when you multiply two integers. The rules for finding the quotient of two integers match the rules for finding the product.

Signs of Integers   **Answer is:**

Multiply → Same sign → +
or
Divide → Different signs → −

If the number you are dividing is 0, the quotient is 0.
You cannot use 0 as a divisor.

Example

Divide.

a. $18 \div (-6) = -3$ The integers have different signs, so the quotient is negative.

b. $-40 \div (-5) = 8$ The integers have the same sign, so the quotient is positive.

c. $0 \div (-4) = 0$ The number being divided is 0, so the quotient is 0.

d. $-49 \div 7 = -7$ The integers have different signs, so the quotient is negative.

Guided Practice

Tell whether the quotient is positive, negative, or 0. Then divide.

1. $-35 \div 7$

The integers have different signs.

The quotient is _____.

So, $-35 \div 7 =$ _____.

2. $-54 \div (-9)$

The integers have the same sign.

The quotient is _____.

So, $-54 \div (-9) =$ _____.

3. $100 \div (-2)$

The integers have different signs.

The quotient is _____.

So, $100 \div (-2) =$ _____.

4. $0 \div (-8)$

The integer being divided is 0.

The quotient is _____.

So, $0 \div (-8) =$ _____.

© Prentice-Hall, Inc.

SKILL 7: Practice

Tell whether the quotient is positive, negative, or 0. Then divide.

1. 72 ÷ (−8)

_____

72 ÷ (−8) = _____

2. −45 ÷ (−9)

_____

−45 ÷ (−9) = _____

3. 35 ÷ 5

_____

35 ÷ 5 = _____

4. 0 ÷ 2

_____

0 ÷ 2 = _____

5. −42 ÷ 7

_____

−42 ÷ 7 = _____

6. −36 ÷ (−6)

_____

−36 ÷ (−6) = _____

Divide.

7. −8 ÷ (−4) = _____

8. −20 ÷ 4 = _____

9. −6 ÷ 2 = _____

10. −12 ÷ 3 = _____

11. −5 ÷ 5 = _____

12. −18 ÷ 3 = _____

13. −45 ÷ (−5) = _____

14. −4 ÷ (−1) = _____

15. −48 ÷ 6 = _____

16. −6 ÷ (−2) = _____

17. 0 ÷ (−5) = _____

18. 12 ÷ (−6) = _____

19. 56 ÷ 8 = _____

20. −35 ÷ (−7) = _____

21. 48 ÷ (−8) = _____

22. 72 ÷ (−8) = _____

23. −45 ÷ (−9) = _____

24. −35 ÷ 5 = _____

25. −42 ÷ 7 = _____

26. 0 ÷ 2 = _____

27. −36 ÷ (−6) = _____

28. 18 ÷ (−2) = _____

29. −20 ÷ (−20) = _____

30. 0 ÷ (−16) = _____

Solve.

31. The total change in the price of a share of stock over a
5-day period was −$15. If the price went down by the same
amount each day, what was the change in price each day?   _____

32. Mario's weight increased by 18 pounds over 3 years. If the
increase was the same each year, how much weight did
Mario gain each year?   _____

33. Find −64 ÷ (−8).

Skill 7

A −8   **C** 6

B −6   **D** 8

34. Find 6 − (−10).

Skill 5

F −16   **H** 4

G −4   **J** 16

SKILL 8: PROBLEM SOLVING:
Operations with Integers

Integers are often used to solve problems that involve increases and decreases, gains and losses, or other quantities that may be greater than or less than zero.

Example

A computer store lowered the price of a laptop computer $45 each month. The store did this over a 6-month period. What was the change in price over this period of time?

Read The price of the laptop decreased by $45 each month. This happened 6 different times.

Plan What integers describe the situation? The negative integer −45 can be used to represent a *decrease* of $45. The positive integer 6 represents the number of times the price was lowered. Since the change represented by −45 occurred 6 times, multiply −45 by 6.

Solve Find 6 · (−45). You are multiplying integers that have different signs, so the product will be negative.

6 · (−45) = −270

There was a change of −$270 in the price of the laptop computer.

Look Back Does your answer makes sense? The price changed by almost $50 in each of 6 months. The number of dollars by which the price changed was almost $300. Since $270 is close to $300, and since the change was a decrease, the answer, −$270, makes sense.

Guided Practice

1. A football team made a 15-yard gain on one play. On the next play, the team had an 8-yard loss. What was the total change? Was it an overall gain or loss?

   a. The gain can be represented by the integer _____.

   b. The loss can be represented by the integer _____.

   c. The total change was _____ yards.

   d. Since the total change is a positive integer, the team had an overall _____.

Name _____ Date _____ Class _____

SKILL 8: Practice

Use integers to solve each problem.

1. In January, Doreen's bank balance decreased by $50. In February, her balance increased by $30. What was the total change in her balance? _____

2. Mr. Schultz wanted to write a check for $85. He noticed that he had only $80 in his checking account. What integer shows what Mr. Schultz's checking account balance would have been if he had written the check? _____

3. In golf, a score of 0 is called *even par*. One *over par* is represented by +1 and one *under par* is represented by −1. In a golf competition, a player had scores of +2, +1, −2, and 0. What was the player's total score? _____

4. Maria's score changes in a video game were +80, −90, and +40. What was the total change? _____

5. The price of a share of stock dropped $35 over a 5-day period. The change in price was the same on each of the 5 days. What was the change in price each day? _____

6. On a test, the teacher gave +10 points for each correct answer, 0 points for a skipped question, and −5 points for each incorrect answer. There were 10 questions on the test. Alex had 8 correct answers and 2 incorrect answers. What score did Alex get? _____

7. A mountain climber reached the top of a mountain that was 10,000 ft above sea level. After descending 3,400 ft, he rested for an hour. What was the level at which he rested? _____

8. In a science experiment, the temperature of a liquid dropped 30° over 6 hours. What integer shows the average hourly temperature change of the liquid? _____

9. The temperature in Bensonville dropped 3°F each hour for 4 hours. What was the total temperature change over the 4-hour period?

Skill 8

   A −12°F   **C** 7°F
   B −7°F   **D** 12°F

10. Find −48 ÷ (−6).

Skill 7

   F 9   **H** −8
   G 8   **J** −9

TEST PREP FOR SECTION A

Circle each correct answer.

1. What integer is the opposite of 14?

   Skill 1

   A −41   **C** 0

   B −14   **D** 41

2. Which list shows the integers −3, 7, −4, and −9 in order from least to greatest?

   Skill 3

   F −9, −4, −3, 7

   G −3, −4, −9, 7

   H −9, 7, −4, −3

   J −3, −4, 7, −9

3. Add: 7 + (−4).

   Skill 4

   A −11   **C** 3

   B −3   **D** 11

4. What is the value of $|-8|$?

   Skill 2

   F 8   **H** 0

   G 4   **J** −8

5. The temperature at 6 A.M. was −14°F. By 10 A.M. the temperature had increased 5°F. What was the temperature at 10 A.M.?

   Skill 8

   A 19°F   **C** −8°F

   B 9°F   **D** −9°F

6. Multiply: −8 × 9.

   Skill 6

   F 72   **H** −17

   G 17   **J** −72

7. Divide: −100 ÷ (−5).

   Skill 7

   A −25   **C** 20

   B −20   **D** 25

8. Write the subtraction problem −5 − (−8) as an addition problem.

   Skill 5

   F 5 + 8   **H** −5 − $|-8|$

   G −5 + 8   **J** 5 + (−8)

9. Add: −8 + (−6).

   Skill 4

   A −14   **C** 2

   B −2   **D** 14

10. Subtract: −5 − (−3).

    Skill 5

    F 2   **H** 8

    G −2   **J** −8

11. What is the value of $|20|$?

    Skill 2

    A −40   **C** 0

    B −20   **D** 20

12. Divide −48 ÷ 6.

    Skill 7

    F −9   **H** 8

    G −8   **J** 9

13. Subtract: 4 − (−4).

    Skill 5

    A 0   **C** −8

    B 8   **D** 4

Mixed Review for Section A

What did the algebra teacher say when asked what she thought about negative numbers?

To find out, locate the answer to each exercise in the code. Write the letter for the exercise in the blank above the exercise number. One letter in the code is not used.

1. negative integer with

   absolute value 7 _____

2. positive integer

   less than 2 _____

3. opposite

   of -3 _____

4. $8 + (-4) =$ _____

5. $\left|-6\right| =$ _____

6. $-6 \cdot 3 =$ _____

7. $-5 - 7 =$ _____

8. $5 - 7 =$ _____

9. $63 \div 7 =$ _____

10. $-30 \div 5 =$ _____

11. $-8 \cdot (-1) =$ _____

12. $-4 - (-3) =$ _____

13. $\left|10\right| =$ _____

14. $8 + (-11) =$ _____

15. $9 + (-7) =$ _____

16. $-49 \div (-7) =$ _____

17. $5 + (-9) =$ _____

18. $\left|-12\right| =$ _____

19. $56 \div (-7) =$ _____

20. $-27 \div 3 =$ _____

21. $70 + (-80) =$ _____

F	T	I	P	S	E	S	N	I	A	Y
-18	6	-3	1	-10	9	3	-7	-8	-12	12

O	K	L	A	I	C	V	T	N	I	G
2	5	10	-6	7	-9	8	-4	-2	4	-1

The algebra teacher said, "I think negative numbers are

___ ___ ___ ___ ___ ___ ___ ___ ___ ___
2 15 3 4 5 16 11 9 13 18

___ ___ ___ ___ ___ ___ ___ ___ ___ ___ ___!"
6 7 21 20 19 1 10 17 14 8 12

SKILL 9: Order of Operations

To make sure everyone gets the same result when calculating the value of an expression, mathematicians use a set of rules known as the **order of operations**.

Order of Operations

1. Multiply and divide in order from left to right.

2. Add and subtract in order from left to right.

Example 1

Simplify: $20 + 3 \cdot (-4)$.

Follow the order of operations.

$20 + 3 \cdot (-4)$ Multiply first.

       $\downarrow$

$20 + \;\; (-12) = 8$ Add.

So, $20 + 3 \cdot (-4) = 8$.

Example 2

Simplify: $-48 \div 8 - 10 \cdot 9$.

Follow the order of operations.

$-48 \div 8 - 10 \cdot 9$ Divide: $-48 \div 8$. Multiply: $10 \cdot 9$.

     $\downarrow$ $\downarrow$

    $-6 \;\; - \;\; 90 = -96$ Subtract.

So, $-48 \div 8 - 10 \cdot 9 = -96$.

Guided Practice

Simplify by completing each step.

1. Simplify: $72 \div 9 \cdot 4 + 5$.

$= \underline{\hspace{2em}} \cdot 4 + 5$

$= \underline{\hspace{2em}} + 5$

$= \underline{\hspace{2em}}$

2. Simplify: $7 + (-3) \cdot 2 - 8 \div 4$.

$= 7 + (\underline{\hspace{2em}}) - 8 \div 4$

$= 7 + (\underline{\hspace{2em}}) - \underline{\hspace{2em}}$

$= \underline{\hspace{2em}} - \underline{\hspace{2em}}$

$= \underline{\hspace{2em}}$

SKILL 9: Practice

Simplify.

1. $9 + 2 \cdot 3 =$ _____

2. $8 + 4 \cdot (-2) =$ _____

3. $7 - 24 \div 8 =$ _____

4. $20 \div 2 - 24 \div 3 =$ _____

5. $5 \cdot 3 + 5 \cdot 2 =$ _____

6. $15 - 30 \div 5 =$ _____

7. $9 + 3 \cdot 6 - 4 =$ _____

8. $-4 + 6 \cdot 7 =$ _____

9. $10 - 3 \cdot 5 =$ _____

10. $12 - 3 \cdot 2 + 30 =$ _____

11. $-8 + 16 \div (-4) =$ _____

12. $10 - 18 \div (-2) + 4 =$ _____

13. $17 - 9 \cdot 3 =$ _____

14. $1 + 3 \cdot 2 \cdot 4 =$ _____

15. $8 + 3 \cdot 4 + 10 \div 5 =$ _____

16. $25 + 3 \cdot 6 \div 2 =$ _____

17. $3 \cdot 2 - 16 =$ _____

18. $1 - 8 \div 4 \div 2 =$ _____

19. $3 + (-4) \cdot 6 =$ _____

20. $6 - 8 \div 2 - 10 =$ _____

21. $-2 + (-3) \cdot (-1) =$ _____

22. $12 + 14 \div 7 =$ _____

23. $19 + - 3 \cdot 4 - 2 \cdot 3 =$ _____

24. $20 \div 2 - 24 \div 3 =$ _____

Solve.

25. The temperature was 78°F at 3 P.M. Each hour for the next 4 hours, the temperature decreased by 3°F. What was the temperature at 7 P.M.? _____

26. Max had a score of −700 points in a video game. On each of the next 3 plays, he gained 400 points. Then what was his score? _____

27. Simplify: $8 + 16 \div (-2)$.   *Skill 9*

   A 16   **C** 0

   B 12   **D** −12

28. Add: $23 + (-9)$.   *Skill 4*

   F −14   **H** 24

   G 14   **J** 32

SKILL 10: Translating Words to Algebraic Expressions

A **variable** is a letter or other symbol that stands for a number. An **expression** is made up of numbers, variables, and/or operation symbols. Some words can be translated into specific mathematical or algebraic expressions.

Word	Definition	Expressions	
sum	The result of **adding** numbers	$7 + 2$	$8 + x$
difference	The result of **subtracting** numbers	$12 - 3$	$28 - y$
product	The result of **multiplying** numbers	4×16	$8c$ or $8 \cdot c$
quotient	The result of **dividing** numbers	$81 \div 9$	$\frac{14}{s}$ or $14 \div s$

To translate situations that don't use these words, you need to choose an operation that is appropriate for the situation. It may be easier to choose an operation if you first replace the variable with a number.

Example

Write an expression to answer: What is the quotient of 99 divided by *x*?

Step 1 What operation is being done?

A quotient is the answer when dividing, so use division to write the expression.

Step 2 Use the appropriate operation sign to write the expression.

$99 \div x$ or $\frac{99}{x}$

The expressions $99 \div x$ and $\frac{99}{x}$ show the quotient of 99 divided by *x*.

Guided Practice

Write an expression to answer each question.

1. What is 12 minus *r*?

  a. What operation is being done? _____

  b. Write the expression. _____

2. What is 32 times as large as *y*?

  a. What operation is being done? _____

  b. Write the expression. _____

3. What is *g* increased by 10?

  a. What operation is being done? _____

  b. Write the expression. _____

4. What is 24 more than *n*? _____

5. What is 11 less than *b*? _____

6. What is *d* divided by 5? _____

SKILL 10: Practice

Write the phrase as an expression.

1. 12 more than x _____

2. x less than 36 _____

3. 2 times 23 _____

4. 17 times s _____

5. b multiplied by 5 _____

6. y decreased by 10 _____

7. 64 plus k _____

8. u tripled _____

9. p divided by 8 _____

10. 18 minus x _____

11. 4 less than k _____

12. z increased by 12 _____

Write an expression to answer each question.

13. What is the product of 82 and g? _____

14. What is the difference between n and 7? _____

15. What is the quotient of 32 and x? _____

16. What is the sum of h and 7? _____

17. Carolyn makes t batches of 12 cookies. How many cookies did she make? _____

18. A jar holds n ounces of jam. How many jars are needed for 100 ounces of jam? _____

19. Brian had p pencils. Then he bought 4 more. How many does he have now? _____

20. Tammy plants 6 rows of t tomato plants each. How many tomato plants did she plant? _____

TEST PREP

21. Which expression means d less than 17?

Skill 10

A $d - 17$ C $d \div 17$

B $17 - d$ D $17 \div d$

22. Simplify: $7 \cdot 6 - 7 \cdot 2$.

Skill 9

F 70   H 28

G 38   J -14

SKILL 11: Evaluating Algebraic Expressions

Expressions such as $-3n$, $x + 2$, and $6 - \square$ that contain variables are called **algebraic expressions**. The value of an algebraic expression depends on the value of each variable in the expression. You can **evaluate** expressions after replacing each variable with a value. This is known as *substituting* a value for the variable. An expression with numbers but without variables is called a **numerical expression.**

Example 1

Evaluate 7d for d = 3.

Replace d with 3. The expression becomes $7 \cdot 3$. Multiply: $7 \cdot 3 = 21$.

So, when you evaluate $7d$ for $d = 3$, the result is 21.

Example 2

Evaluate 3 + 2x, for x = −1.

Replace x with 21. The expression becomes: $3 + 2(-1)$.

Use order of operations to simplify. Multiply first. $3 + (-2)$

Then add.   1

So, when you evaluate $3 + 2x$, for $x = -1$, the result is 1.

Guided Practice

Evaluate the expression by completing the steps.

1. Evaluate $18 - x$ for $x = 7$.

   a. Replace x with its value: $18 -$ _____.

   b. Subtract: $18 -$ _____ $=$ _____.

   c. So, when you evaluate $18 - x$ for $x = 7$, the result is _____.

2. Evaluate $3 + 4y$ for $y = -2$.

   a. Remember that $4y$ means $4 \cdot y$. Replace y with its value: $3 + 4 \cdot ($_____$)$.

   b. Use order of operations to simplify. $3 + ($_____$) =$ _____.

   c. So, when you evaluate $3 + 4y$ for $y = -2$, the result is _____.

SKILL 11: Practice

Evaluate each algebraic expression for the given value of the variable.

1. $12 + x$ for $x = 4$ _____

2. $20 - k$ for $k = 9$ _____

3. $24 \div n$ for $n = 8$ _____

4. $6t$ for $t = 2$ _____

5. $32 - m$ for $m = -3$ _____

6. $h + (-10)$ for $h = 2$ _____

7. $-3j$ for $j = 9$ _____

8. $p \div (-5)$ for $p = 35$ _____

9. $26 + 2x$ for $x = 7$ _____

10. $30 - 4y$ for $y = 8$ _____

11. $20c \div 10$ for $c = 3$ _____

12. $-3m$ for $m = -11$ _____

13. $6 - 3f$ for $f = 6$ _____

14. $2p - 14$ for $p = 13$ _____

15. $-4 + 8t$ for $t = -5$ _____

16. $100 \div j$ for $j = 5$ _____

17. $3k - 8k$ for $k = 16$ _____

18. $-3m + 15 - m$ for $m = 25$ _____

19. $64g \div 8$ for $g = -7$ _____

20. $200 + k \div 9$ for $k = 63$ _____

21. $2y + 8$ for $y = -3$ _____

22. $18 - 3m$ for $m = -1$ _____

23. $\frac{6}{2n}$ for $n = -3$ _____

24. $9z + 2z$ for $z = -2$ _____

Solve.

25. Mark drives $65t$ miles in t hours. How far does
he drive in 2 hours? _____

26. Josefina spent $20 + 3b$ dollars on a pair of earrings
and three blouses that cost b dollars each. How much
did she spend in all if each blouse cost \$15? _____

27. Evaluate $9 + x$ for $x = -3$.

Skill 11

   A -27 **C** 6

   B -12 **D** 12

28. Doug bought a book for
d dollars and a poster for \$8.
What expression represents
how much he spent?

Skill 10

   F $8 + d$ **H** $8d$

   G $d - 8$ **J** $8 \div d$

SKILL 12: Order of Operations with Parentheses

When simplifying expressions containing parentheses,
use the following order of operations:

1. Do operations inside parentheses.

2. Multiply and divide in order from left to right.

3. Add and subtract in order from left to right.

An expression in parentheses is often written
beside a number, a variable, or another expression
in parentheses. When no operation sign is written
between the parentheses and the other part of the
expression, the operation is multiplication.

$3(-2 + 5)$ means $3 \cdot (-2 + 5)$

Example 1

Simplify: $5(-16 + 10)$.

$5(-16 + 10)$

$= \quad 5(-6)$ Do the operation inside the parentheses first.

$= \quad -30$ Then multiply: $5(-6) = -30$.

So, $5(-16 + 10) = -30$.

Example 2

Simplify: $(1 + 2 \cdot 3)(4 - 6)$.

$(1 + 2 \cdot 3)(4 - 6)$

$= (1 + 6)(-2)$ Do the operations in parentheses.

$= \quad (7)(-2)$

$= \quad -14$ Then multiply: $(7)(-2) = -14$.

So, $(1 + 2 \cdot 3)(4 - 6) = -14$.

Guided Practice

Simplify each expression.

1. $6(24 - 14) = 6 \,(\underline{\hspace{2cm}})$

$= \underline{\hspace{2cm}}$

2. $5(7 - 3 \cdot 9) = 5(7 - \underline{\hspace{2cm}})$

$= 5(\underline{\hspace{2cm}})$

$= \underline{\hspace{2cm}}$

SKILL 12: Practice

Simplify each expression.

1. $7(3 + 5) =$ _____

2. $(16 + 4) \div 5 =$ _____

3. $(-2)(3 + 8) =$ _____

4. $(-3 + 9) \div 2 =$ _____

5. $(6 + 4)(2 + 3) =$ _____

6. $3(2 \cdot 5 - 7) =$ _____

7. $(12 \cdot 3 - 1) \div 5 =$ _____

8. $(-8 - 22) \div 10 =$ _____

9. $(-2 + 6)(5 - 8) =$ _____

10. $(13 - 6)(13 - 7) =$ _____

11. $(6 - 13)(7 - 13) =$ _____

12. $18 \div (4 + 5) =$ _____

13. $36 \div (2 - 8) =$ _____

14. $60(8 - 12 + 2) =$ _____

15. $48 \div (2 - 8 \cdot 1) =$ _____

16. $(-9)(15 - 5) =$ _____

17. $54 \div (7 - 13) =$ _____

18. $1 + (3 - 9) + 8 =$ _____

19. $(14 + 10) \div (2 - 6) =$ _____

20. $(4 - 7)(2 + 9) =$ _____

21. $(7 - 6) + (2 - 3 \cdot 4) =$ _____

22. $9 \div (-2 - 1) =$ _____

23. $16 - (5 - 8) =$ _____

24. $(2 \cdot 6 - 4) \div (4 - 8) =$ _____

Solve.

25. The high temperature on Monday was 78°F. The high temperature on Tuesday and Wednesday was 81°F. Evaluate $(78 + 2 \cdot 81) \div 3$ to find the average high temperature for the 3 days.

_____

26. Harry made deposits of $55 and $35 in his bank account. He wrote checks for $20 and $35. Evaluate $(55 + 35) - (20 + 35)$ to find the change in his bank account balance.

_____

27. Evaluate: $2(8 - 12)$.

Skill 12

A 8 **C** −4

B 4 **D** −8

28. Evaluate $7m$ for $m = -2$.

Skill 11

F −14 **H** 5

G −5 **J** 14

Section B: Expressions and Equations

SKILL 13: Solving 1-Step Equations

To solve an equation, you "undo" operations until the variable is alone on one side of the equation. Remember that addition and subtraction undo each other, and multiplication and division undo each other. Also recall that you can use a fraction to show division. To check the solution, substitute the solution for the variable in the equation.

Example 1

Solve: $x + 7 = 18$.

$x + 7 = 18$

$x + 7 - 7 = 18 - 7$ Undo addition by subtracting. Subtract 7 from both sides.

$x = 11$

Check: $11 + 7 \overset{?}{=} 18$

$18 = 18$

The solution is 11.

Example 2

Solve: $5x = -15$.

$5x = -15$

$\dfrac{5x}{5} = \dfrac{-15}{5}$ Undo multiplication by dividing. Divide both sides by 5.

$x = -3$

Check: $5(-3) \overset{?}{=} -15$

$-15 = -15$

The solution is -3.

Guided Practice

Solve each equation. Check your solution.

1. $x - 3 = 10$

$x - 3 + \underline{\hspace{1em}} = 10 + \underline{\hspace{1em}}$

$x = \underline{\hspace{1em}}$

Check:

$\underline{\hspace{2em}} - 3 \overset{?}{=} 10$

$\underline{\hspace{2em}} = \underline{\hspace{2em}}$

The solution is $\underline{\hspace{2em}}$.

2. $8x = -16$

$\dfrac{8x}{8} = \dfrac{-16}{8}$

$x = \underline{\hspace{2em}}$

Check:

$8(\underline{\hspace{2em}}) \overset{?}{=} -16$

$\underline{\hspace{2em}} = \underline{\hspace{2em}}$

The solution is $\underline{\hspace{2em}}$.

3. $\dfrac{x}{7} = 9$

$\dfrac{x}{7}(\underline{\hspace{2em}}) = 9(\underline{\hspace{2em}})$

$x = \underline{\hspace{2em}}$

Check:

$\dfrac{63}{7} \overset{?}{=} 9$

$\underline{\hspace{2em}} = \underline{\hspace{2em}}$

The solution is $\underline{\hspace{2em}}$.

SKILL 13: Practice

Solve each equation.

1. $x + 6 = 14$

$x =$ _____

2. $x + 9 = 19$

$x =$ _____

3. $x - 3 = 7$

$x =$ _____

4. $2x = 18$

$x =$ _____

5. $\frac{n}{5} = 9$

$n =$ _____

6. $(-4)x = 20$

$x =$ _____

7. $m - 10 = -6$

$m =$ _____

8. $\frac{k}{-8} = 6$

$k =$ _____

9. $10x = -70$

$x =$ _____

10. $n - (-8) = 15$

$n =$ _____

11. $-4x = -60$

$x =$ _____

12. $8p = -96$

$p =$ _____

13. $\frac{n}{-11} = 8$

$n =$ _____

14. $x + (-6) = 9$

$x =$ _____

15. $-7k = -63$

$k =$ _____

16. $x + 23 = 37$

$x =$ _____

17. $x - 13 = -28$

$x =$ _____

18. $\frac{m}{-9} = 20$

$m =$ _____

19. $\frac{k}{-6} = -12$

$k =$ _____

20. $12y = -84$

$y =$ _____

21. $m + (-15) = 30$

$m =$ _____

22. $x - (-13) = 2$

$x =$ _____

23. $\frac{n}{3} = -14$

$n =$ _____

24. $-8x = -168$

$x =$ _____

Solve.

25. In a video game, Charles scored −250 points on his second play. This brought his total score to 500. What was his score on the first play? _____

26. Each day for several days, the change in the price of a share of stock was −$3. The total change in price during those days was −$36. Over how many days did the price decline? _____

27. What is the solution of $4x = -28$?

Skill 13

A 24   C −24

B −7   D −32

28. Evaluate: $-4(9 + 5)$.

Skill 12

F 56   H −41

G 41   J −56

Section B: Expressions and Equations

SKILL 14: Solving 2-Step Equations

In some equations, more than one operation is used. To undo the operations, you reverse the original order of operations.

Example

Solve: $3x - 1 = -7$.

In the equation, x was first multiplied by 3 and then 1 was subtracted. To undo the operations, you work backward by first adding 1 and then dividing by 3.

$$3x - 1 = -7$$

Step 1 *Add 1* to each side.

$$3x - 1 + \mathbf{1} = -7 + \mathbf{1}$$
$$3x = -6$$

Step 2 *Divide by 3* on each side.

$$\frac{3x}{3} = \frac{-6}{3}$$
$$x = -2$$

Check: $3(-2) - 1 \overset{?}{=} -7$
$$-6 - 1 \overset{?}{=} -7$$
$$-7 = -7$$

So, the solution is -2.

Guided Practice

Solve each equation.

1. $\frac{x}{-3} + 5 = 9$

$\frac{x}{-3} + 5 -$ _____ $= 9 -$ _____

$\frac{x}{-3} =$ _____

$\frac{x}{-3} \cdot ($ _____ $) = 4 \cdot ($ _____ $)$

$x =$ _____

2. $5x - 7 = 3$

$5x - 7 +$ _____ $= 3 +$ _____

$5x =$ _____

$\frac{5x}{\square} = \frac{10}{\square}$

$x =$ _____

3. $2x + 1 = 13$

$2x + 1 -$ _____ $= 13 -$ _____

$2x =$ _____

$\frac{2x}{\square} = \frac{12}{\square}$

$x =$ _____

4. $\frac{x}{4} - 6 = 3$

$\frac{x}{4} - 6 +$ _____ $= 3 +$ _____

$\frac{x}{4} =$ _____

$\frac{x}{4} \cdot$ _____ $= 9 \cdot$ _____

$x =$ _____

© Prentice-Hall, Inc.

SKILL 14: Practice

To solve each equation, tell what you will do first to both sides.

1. $2x + 7 = 13$

_____

2. $-3n - 8 = 7$

_____

3. $2x - 9 = 11$

_____

4. $-5x + 6 = 36$

_____

5. $10x + (-9) = 21$

_____

6. $4x - 13 = 3$

_____

7. $-5m + 12 = -9$

_____

8. $8k - 11 = 13$

_____

9. $-6n - (-2) = 8$

_____

Solve each equation. Check your solutions.

10. $3b + (-7) = -25$

$b =$ _____

11. $\frac{n}{-4} + (-3) = 8$

$n =$ _____

12. $16 = 4h - 12$

$h =$ _____

13. $\frac{x}{6} - (-10) = 3$

$x =$ _____

14. $8w - 17 = -89$

$w =$ _____

15. $\frac{c}{7} - 12 = -4$

$c =$ _____

16. $\frac{p}{-5} + 12 = 20$

$p =$ _____

17. $5j + (-16) = -76$

$j =$ _____

18. $\frac{k}{-3} + (-8) = -8$

$k =$ _____

For each problem, write an equation. Then solve.

19. Linda had $15 in her coin bank. On her birthday, 5 relatives sent her money as a birthday gift. Each relative sent the same amount. She then had $115. How much money did Linda receive from each relative?

_____

20. Gorillas and chimpanzees can learn sign language to communicate with humans. By 1982, a gorilla named Koko had learned 700 words. This is 50 fewer than 5 times as many words as a chimpanzee named Washoe knew 10 years earlier. How many words did Washoe know?

_____

21. Solve: $4x - 8 = 32$.

Skill 14

A 10   **C** 6

B 8   **D** −6

22. Solve: $n + 15 = 22$.

Skill 13

F −8   **H** 7

G −7   **J** 17

         Section B: Expressions and Equations

SKILL 15: The Coordinate Plane

The **x-y coordinate plane** is based on two number lines. The horizontal line is the **x-axis**, and the vertical line is the **y-axis**. They intersect at the zero point on each number line. This point is called the **origin**. The axes divide the plane into four **quadrants**.

Any point, *P*, can be described by an **ordered pair**. The first number, the **x-coordinate**, tells how far to the left (for a negative number) or to the right (for a positive number) of the origin the point is. The **y-coordinate** tells how far up (for a positive number) or down (for a negative number) the point is. The origin is at (0, 0).

Example 1

What point is described by (−3, 4)?

Move left 3 units.

(−3, 4)

Move up 4 units.

(−3, 4) describes point *A*.

Example 2

Find the coordinates of point *B*.

Point *B* is located 5 units to the left of the origin (−5 on the *x*-axis) and 3 units down (−3 on the *y*-axis).

So, the coordinates of point *B* are (−5, −3).

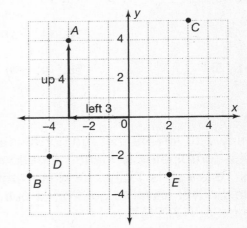

Guided Practice

Refer to the diagram to the right of Examples 1 and 2.

1. What point is described by (−4, −2)?

Start at the origin.

Move _____ 4 units,
　　　　(left/right)

then move _____ 2 units.
　　　　　　　(up/down)

You come to point ____.

2. What are the coordinates of point *C*?

Start at the origin. To get to point *C*,

move _____ _____ units, then
　　　(left/right)　(how many?)

move _____ _____ units. The
　　　(up/down)　(how many?)

coordinates of point *C* are (____, ____).

SKILL 15: Practice

Find the coordinates of each point.

1. S _____

2. T _____

3. U _____

4. V _____

5. W _____

6. X _____

7. Y _____

8. Z _____

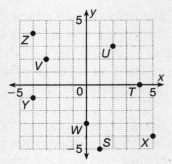

Name the point that has the given coordinates.

9. (2, −4) _____

10. (0, 4) _____

11. (−3, 2) _____

12. (0, 0) _____

13. (−2, 0) _____

14. (−1, −3) _____

15. (5, 3) _____

16. (4, −1) _____

17. (−5, 5) _____

18. (4, −3) _____

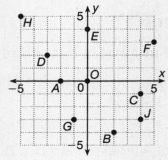

Solve.

19. A city with streets that run north/south and east/west
    uses coordinates to identify locations of buildings. The
    unit of length is 1 city block. How many blocks must
    a taxi driver travel to get from a bus stop at (2, 5) to a
    house at (17, 25)?

    _____

20. What are the coordinates of
    a point in the coordinate plane
    that is 2 units to the right of the
    origin and 7 units down?

    Skill 15

    A (−2, −7)   **C** (2, −7)

    B (−2, 7)   **D** (2, 7)

21. Solve: $6x + 5 = -13$.

    Skill 14

    F −18   **H** 3

    G −3   **J** 18

Section B: Expressions and Equations

Circle each correct answer.

1. Evaluate $30 - 2k$ for $k = -8$.

Skill 11

  A 46   **C** 20

  B 40   **D** 14

2. Simplify: $6 - 21 \div 3$.

Skill 9

  F 45   **H** -1

  G 1   **J** -45

3. Solve: $-5m = 45$.

Skill 13

  A -40 **C** 9

  B -9 **D** 40

4. Write an expression to answer: What is the sum of h and 73?

Skill 10

  F $73h$ **H** $h + 73$

  G $73 - h$ **J** $h \cdot 73$

5. Simplify: $60 \div (2 + 4)$.

Skill 12

  A 10   **C** 45

  B 34   **D** 55

6. Solve: $\frac{m}{4} + 10 = 7$.

Skill 14

  F -68 **H** 12

  G -12 **J** 68

7. Simplify: $2(8 - 2 \cdot 4)$.

Skill 12

  A 8   **C** 0

  B 48   **D** 56

8. Solve: $x - 5 = -10$.

Skill 13

  F -5 **H** 5

  G -15 **J** 15

9. What are the coordinates of point M?

Skill 15

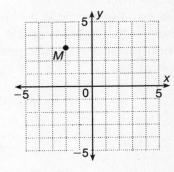

  A $(-3, 2)$ **C** $(-2, -3)$

  B $(-3, -2)$ **D** $(-2, 3)$

10. Simplify: $(8 + 12) \div (-3 + 1)$.

Skill 12

  F 10   **H** -5

  G 5   **J** -10

11. Write an expression to answer: What is -19 decreased by y?

Skill 10

  A $y - (-19)$ **C** $-19 \div y$

  B $-19 - y$ **D** $y \div (-19)$

12. Solve: $-4w + 6 = 46$.

Skill 14

  F -13 **H** 10

  G -10 **J** 13

Mixed Review for Section B

One day, a complicated equation, struggling to find its solution, decided to visit a computer. The computer operated on the equation and found the solution rather quickly. How did the computer describe the look on the face of the equation after it was all over?

To find out, answer each exercise. Write the circled code letter on the blank above the answer at the bottom of the page. Use the computer screen diagram for Exercises 5 and 15.

1. Solution of
$b - 50 = 101$

_____ Ⓢ

2. Value of $6 + 5x$
for $x = -2$

_____ Ⓘ

3. Solution of
$8k = -96$

_____ Ⓔ

4. Value of
$7 \cdot (-9) + 9 \div 3 \cdot 4$

_____ Ⓞ

5. Ordered pair
for point M

_____ Ⓐ

6. Value of $\frac{r}{3}$
for $r = 90$

_____ Ⓔ

7. Expression for
43 less than n

_____ Ⓓ

8. Value of
$4(-12 + 7 \cdot 3)$

_____ Ⓟ

9. Solution of
$10k + 12 = 32$

_____ Ⓔ

10. Value of
$5(3 \cdot 8 - 30)$

_____ Ⓓ

11. Solution of
$\frac{m}{-16} = -9$

_____ Ⓧ

12. Solution of
$-11w + 6 = -38$

_____ Ⓢ

13. Value of
$9 - 2 \cdot 8$

_____ Ⓡ

14. Expression for
50 more than h

_____ Ⓩ

15. Letter formed by joining
$(-1, 2)$ to $(1, -2)$
and $(-1, -2)$ to $(1, 2)$

_____ Ⓝ

_____ _____ _____ _____ _____
$n - 43$ $(-3, -2)$ $h + 50$ 2 -30

_____ _____ _____ _____ _____ _____ _____ _____ _____
-12 144 36 -7 30 4 151 -4 -51 X

SKILL 16: Defining and Comparing Rational Numbers

Rational numbers are numbers that can be written as a ratio of two integers. The denominator can not be zero. Some examples of rational numbers are $\frac{-2}{3}$, $\frac{5}{8}$, $\frac{12}{-7}$, and $\frac{47}{100}$.

Some numbers that at first might not look like rational numbers actually are rational numbers, because they can be written as equivalent fractions with numerators and denominators that are integers. For example, $-\frac{3}{5} = \frac{-3}{5}$, $1.25 = \frac{5}{4}$, and $-0.\overline{3} = \frac{-1}{3}$.

Example 1

> **Show that each number is a rational number by writing an equivalent fraction with a numerator and a denominator that are both integers.**
>
> **a.** $-4\frac{1}{6}$
>
> $-4\frac{1}{6} = -\frac{25}{6} = \frac{-25}{6}$
>
> So $-4\frac{1}{6}$ is a rational number.
>
> **b.** -0.125
>
> $-0.125 = -\frac{125}{1,000} = \frac{-1}{8}$
>
> So -0.125 is a rational number.

You can compare rational numbers in much the same way as you compare fractions, decimals, and integers.

Example 2

> **Compare $-1\frac{3}{5}$ and $-2\frac{1}{2}$.**
>
> Write the rational numbers using the positive common denominator 10.
>
> $-1\frac{3}{5} = \frac{-8}{5} = \frac{-16}{10}$ $-2\frac{1}{2} = \frac{-5}{2} = \frac{-25}{10}$
>
> Compare the numerators. Since $-16 > -25$, you know that $\frac{-16}{10} > \frac{-25}{10}$.
>
> So, $-1\frac{3}{5} > -2\frac{1}{2}$.

Guided Practice

1. Write 4.6 as a ratio of two integers.

$4.6 = 4\frac{\boxed{}}{10} = \frac{\boxed{}}{10}$

2. Compare $-1\frac{4}{5}$ and $\frac{2}{3}$.

Every negative number is _____ (less/greater) than every positive number.

So, $-1\frac{4}{5} \bigcirc \frac{2}{3}$.

SKILL 16: Practice

Write each rational number as a ratio of two integers.

1. $-3\frac{3}{4}$ _____

2. $1\frac{6}{7}$ _____

3. -0.8 _____

4. $-\frac{5}{6}$ _____

5. $-4\frac{2}{5}$ _____

6. $-\frac{34}{35}$ _____

7. 0.55 _____

8. $-1.\overline{3}$ _____

9. $8\frac{2}{3}$ _____

Use >, <, or = to compare the rational numbers.

10. $\frac{2}{3}$ ◯ $\frac{1}{4}$

11. $-\frac{2}{3}$ ◯ $-\frac{3}{4}$

12. $-5\frac{1}{2}$ ◯ $7\frac{1}{2}$

13. $3\frac{1}{5}$ ◯ $-7\frac{2}{5}$

14. $-1\frac{1}{4}$ ◯ $-1\frac{1}{5}$

15. $-\frac{3}{4}$ ◯ $-\frac{3}{8}$

16. -5.5 ◯ $-5\frac{1}{2}$

17. $\frac{2}{3}$ ◯ $-\frac{19}{20}$

18. $-3\frac{7}{8}$ ◯ $-1\frac{5}{6}$

19. $\frac{4}{5}$ ◯ $-12\frac{3}{4}$

20. 0.7 ◯ -0.9

21. 0 ◯ -0.3

22. $-\frac{1}{3}$ ◯ $-0.\overline{3}$

23. $\frac{17}{16}$ ◯ $-\frac{17}{16}$

24. $0.\overline{6}$ ◯ $\frac{2}{3}$

25. $\frac{5}{8}$ ◯ $\frac{3}{32}$

26. $-\frac{16}{3}$ ◯ $-\frac{14}{3}$

27. 0.75 ◯ $\frac{3}{4}$

Solve.

28. On Monday, the temperature went down to $-15°F$ at a weather station in Canada. On Tuesday, the temperature dropped to $-19.5°F$. Which day had the lower temperature? _____

29. Last year, Lucille grew 1.25 inches. Berta grew $1\frac{2}{3}$ inches. Which girl grew more? _____

30. Which number is greater than $-\frac{2}{3}$?

Skill 16

A $-\frac{1}{3}$ **C** $-\frac{4}{5}$

B $-\frac{3}{4}$ **D** -1

31. Find $-7 + 18$.

Skill 4

F -25 **H** 11

G -11 **J** 25

SKILL 17: Computing with Rational Numbers

What you have learned about opposites and absolute value of integers applies to rational numbers also. (The opposite of $\frac{2}{3}$ is $-\frac{2}{3}$, the absolute value of $-\frac{3}{4}$ is $\frac{3}{4}$, and so on.) This means that you can add, subtract, multiply, and divide rational numbers in much the same way you did integers.

Example 1

Add: $-\frac{3}{5} + \frac{1}{5}$.

Rewrite $-\frac{3}{5}$ as $\frac{-3}{5}$.

The denominators are the same. Add the numerators.

$$\frac{-3}{5} + \frac{1}{5} = \frac{-3+1}{5} = \frac{-2}{5}$$

So, $-\frac{3}{5} + \frac{1}{5} = \frac{-2}{5}$ or $-\frac{2}{5}$.

Example 2

Multiply: $-\frac{2}{3} \cdot \left(-\frac{1}{5}\right)$.

Rewrite $-\frac{2}{3}$ as $\frac{-2}{3}$ and $-\frac{1}{5}$ as $\frac{-1}{5}$.

You are multiplying numbers with the same sign, so the answer will be positive.

Multiply the numerators.
Multiply the denominators.

$$\frac{-2}{3} \cdot \frac{-1}{5} = \frac{-2 \cdot (-1)}{3 \cdot 5} = \frac{2}{15}$$

So, $-\frac{2}{3} \cdot \left(-\frac{1}{5}\right) = \frac{2}{15}$.

Guided Practice

1. Subtract: $1.5 - (-12.9)$.

Change subtraction to addition, and add the *opposite* of _____.

$1.5 - (-12.9) = 1.5 +$ _____

$=$ _____

So, $1.5 - (-12.9) =$ _____.

2. Multiply: $7.5 \cdot (-9)$.

$7.5 \cdot 9 =$ _____

Since 7.5 and -9 have different signs, the final answer will be _____.
(negative/positive)

So, $7.5 \cdot (-9) =$ _____.

3. Divide: $-1.5 \div 5$.

Since the numbers -1.5 and 5 have different signs, the answer is _____.
(negative/positive)

$1.5 \div 5 =$ _____   So, $-1.5 \div 5 =$ _____.

SKILL 17: Practice

Add or subtract. Write fractions in simplest form.

1. $8.3 + (-4.1) =$ _____

2. $6 - 9.2 =$ _____

3. $-7.69 - 14.8 =$ _____

4. $\frac{3}{5} + \frac{1}{5} =$ _____

5. $-\frac{15}{11} - \frac{7}{11} =$ _____

6. $-\frac{1}{8} + \frac{3}{8} =$ _____

7. $\frac{5}{12} - \frac{7}{12} =$ _____

8. $-\frac{11}{15} + \frac{7}{15} =$ _____

9. $-\frac{3}{4} - \left(-5\frac{3}{4}\right) =$ _____

10. $8\frac{1}{3} - 9\frac{2}{3} =$ _____

11. $4\frac{5}{6} - 2\frac{1}{6} =$ _____

12. $\frac{5}{12} + \left(-7\frac{11}{12}\right) =$ _____

Multiply or divide. Write fractions in simplest form.

13. $9.16 \cdot (-0.2) =$ _____

14. $7.03 \cdot 0.04 =$ _____

15. $-0.1 \cdot (-4.1) =$ _____

16. $-8.64 \div 2 =$ _____

17. $90.5 \div (-5) =$ _____

18. $-6.4 \div (-0.8) =$ _____

19. $\frac{1}{2} \cdot (-4) =$ _____

20. $-\frac{2}{3} \cdot (-3) =$ _____

21. $-\frac{1}{2} \cdot \frac{3}{4} =$ _____

22. $1\frac{1}{2} \div (-8) =$ _____

23. $3\frac{1}{2} \div 7 =$ _____

24. $-7.5 \div 3 =$ _____

25. $-\frac{3}{8} \cdot \left(-\frac{5}{6}\right) =$ _____

26. $-\frac{3}{5} \div \left(-\frac{7}{8}\right) =$ _____

27. $\frac{4}{5} \cdot (-5) =$ _____

Solve.

28. The area of Colombia is about $1\frac{1}{4}$ times the area of Venezuela, which is about 352,000 square miles. What is the area of Colombia? _____

29. Miguel bought some stock priced at $14\frac{3}{8}$ per share. Find the value of the stock after it went up $2\frac{3}{4}$. _____

30. Add: $\frac{-2}{3} + \frac{1}{3}$.

    A 1   **C** $-\frac{1}{3}$

    B $\frac{1}{3}$ **D** -1

Skill 17

31. Which rational number is greater than $-\frac{3}{5}$?

Skill 16

    F $-\frac{16}{20}$ **H** $-\frac{9}{15}$

    G $-\frac{10}{15}$ **J** $-\frac{2}{15}$

SKILL 18: Solving Equations with Rational Numbers

You can use the same procedures to solve equations with rational numbers that you used to solve equations with integers. You "undo" operations so that the variable is alone on one side of the equation.

Example 1

Solve: $\frac{2}{3}x = -\frac{1}{4}$.

$\frac{2}{3}x = \frac{-1}{4}$ Rewrite $-\frac{1}{4}$ as $\frac{-1}{4}$.

$\frac{2}{3}x \div \frac{2}{3} = \frac{-1}{4} \div \frac{2}{3}$ Undo multiplication by division. Divide both sides by $\frac{2}{3}$.

$x = \frac{-1}{4} \cdot \frac{3}{2}$ Change division by a fraction to multiplication by its reciprocal.

$= \frac{-1 \cdot 3}{4 \cdot 2}$ Multiply numerators. Multiply denominators.

$x = \frac{-3}{8}$

The solution is $-\frac{3}{8}$.

Example 2

Solve: $\frac{x}{-0.4} = 6$.

$\frac{x}{-0.4} = 6$ x is divided by -0.4.

$\frac{x}{-0.4} \cdot (-0.4) = 6 \cdot (-0.4)$ Undo division by multiplication. Multiply both sides by -0.4.

$x = -2.4$

The solution is -2.4.

Guided Practice

Solve each equation. Check your solution.

1. $m - 5 = -\frac{1}{2}$

5 is _____ from m.
(added/subtracted)

Undo this operation by _____.
(addition/subtraction)

$m - 5 + _____ = -\frac{1}{2} + _____$

$x = _____$

2. $-0.6x = -6$

x is multiplied by _____.

Undo multiplication by _____.

$\frac{-0.6x}{-0.6} = \frac{-6}{-0.6}$

$x = _____$

SKILL 18: Practice

Solve each equation. Check your solution.

1. $x + \frac{5}{7} = \frac{6}{7}$ **2.** $x - \frac{1}{8} = -\frac{5}{8}$ **3.** $6m = -\frac{1}{2}$

  $x =$ _____ $x =$ _____ $m =$ _____

4. $k + 4\frac{1}{2} = 3\frac{1}{2}$ **5.** $\frac{n}{-4} = \frac{1}{2}$ **6.** $y - \frac{5}{8} = -\frac{3}{8}$

  $k =$ _____ $n =$ _____ $y =$ _____

7. $-3y = \frac{5}{8}$ **8.** $10x = -7$ **9.** $m + 9 = -11$

  $y =$ _____ $x =$ _____ $m =$ _____

10. $t + \left(-1\frac{1}{2}\right) = -6\frac{1}{2}$ **11.** $j - \left(-4\frac{1}{3}\right) = -10$ **12.** $2k = \frac{1}{8}$

  $t =$ _____ $j =$ _____ $k =$ _____

13. $x - 3.2 = -20.8$ **14.** $-0.25x = 2$ **15.** $\frac{5}{16}n = -10$

  $x =$ _____ $x =$ _____ $n =$ _____

16. $-\frac{4}{5}m = 6$ **17.** $\frac{8}{9}t = -\frac{1}{3}$ **18.** $y + 1\frac{1}{4} = 7\frac{1}{4}$

  $m =$ _____ $t =$ _____ $y =$ _____

19. $-\frac{1}{4}j = \frac{2}{3}$ **20.** $-0.01k = 0.8$ **21.** $-6t = 6.6$

  $j =$ _____ $k =$ _____ $t =$ _____

Solve.

22. The price of a share of stock changed by $-\$19.20$ over a 5-day period. What was the average daily change in the price of a share of the stock?   _____

23. Janice plans to save \$22.50 each week until she has enough money to buy a \$180 bicycle. After how many weeks will she have enough money for the bicycle?   _____

24. Solve $2x = -8.4$.

                                             Skill 18

  A -16.8 **C** 4.2

  B -4.2 **D** -42

25. Multiply: $-\frac{3}{4} \cdot \left(-\frac{2}{3}\right)$.

                                             Skill 17

  F $\frac{1}{2}$ **H** $-\frac{1}{2}$

  G $-\frac{5}{12}$ **J** $1\frac{1}{8}$

SKILL 19: Exponents and Square Roots

Remember that in exponential notation, the **exponent** tells you how many times the base is used as a factor.

$$3 \cdot 3 \cdot 3 \cdot 3 \cdot 3 = 3^5$$

5 is the exponent.

5 factors   **3 is the base.**

3^5 is read as "3 to the fifth power."

Exponential form	Expanded form	Standard form
3^5	$3 \cdot 3 \cdot 3 \cdot 3 \cdot 3$	243
$(0.2)^3$	$0.2 \cdot 0.2 \cdot 0.2$	0.008
$\left(\frac{1}{5}\right)^2$	$\frac{1}{5} \cdot \frac{1}{5}$	$\frac{1}{25}$

Example 1

Write $(-7)^3$ in standard and expanded forms.

$$(-7)^3 = (-7) \cdot (-7) \cdot (-7)$$
$$= 49 \cdot (-7)$$
$$= -343$$

In expanded form, $(-7)^3 = (-7) \cdot (-7) \cdot (-7)$.
In standard form, $(-7)^3 = -343$.

Powers of Negative Numbers
Suppose the base is negative.
If the exponent is an even number, the standard form is positive. If the exponent is an odd number, the standard form is negative.

$$(-2)^3 = -8 \qquad (-2)^4 = 16$$
$$(-2)^5 = -32 \qquad (-2)^6 = 64$$

Finding the **square root** of a number is the inverse of squaring the number.

Squaring 5: $5^2 = 25$ Square root of 25: $\sqrt{25} = 5$.

You can see numbers and their squares in the table at the right. You can also use a calculator.

n	n^2	n	n^2
1	1	11	121
2	4	12	144
3	9	13	169
4	16	14	196
5	25	15	225
6	36	16	256
7	49	17	289
8	64	18	324
9	81	19	361
10	100	20	400

Example 2

Find the square root of 196.
From the table, you know $14^2 = 196$, so $\sqrt{196} = 14$.

Guided Practice

1. Write $(-3)^4$ in expanded and standard forms.

-3 is used as a factor _____ times.

Expanded form: (___) · (___) · (___) · (___).

The exponent is an _____ number.
(even/odd)

The standard form for $(-3)^4$ is _____.

2. Find the square root of 324.

The number to the left of 324 in the table is _____.

$\sqrt{324} =$ _____

SKILL 19: Practice

Write using exponents.

1. $3 \cdot 3 \cdot 3 \cdot 3 \cdot 3 \cdot 3$ _____

2. $10 \cdot 10 \cdot 10 \cdot 10 \cdot 10 \cdot 10 \cdot 10$ _____

3. $(-4) \cdot (-4) \cdot (-4)$ _____

4. $(-8) \cdot (-8) \cdot (-8) \cdot (-8)$ _____

5. $9 \cdot 9$ _____

6. $(-1) \cdot (-1) \cdot (-1)$ _____

Write in expanded form.

7. 1.9^4 _____

8. $(-0.6)^3$ _____

9. 20^5 _____

10. $\left(-\frac{2}{3}\right)^3$ _____

11. 2^6 _____

12. $(-4)^4$ _____

Write in standard form.

13. 4^3 _____

14. 5^4 _____

15. 10^2 _____

16. 10^5 _____

17. $(-2)^5$ _____

18. $(-3)^4$ _____

19. 20^3 _____

20. $(-1)^4$ _____

21. 30^5 _____

22. $(0.02)^3$ _____

23. 45^2 _____

24. $(0.1)^4$ _____

Find each square root.

25. $\sqrt{144}$ _____

26. $\sqrt{81}$ _____

27. $\sqrt{361}$ _____

28. $\sqrt{169}$ _____

29. $\sqrt{225}$ _____

30. $\sqrt{256}$ _____

Solve.

31. Suppose you toss a penny, a nickel, a dime, and a quarter at the same time and record the heads and tails. There are 2^4 ways the coins can land. Write this number in standard form. _____

32. Suppose you roll 3 dice of different colors and record what number you get for each color. There are 6^3 number combinations possible. Write this number in standard form. _____

33. What is $(-2)^4$ in standard form?

Skill 19

A -8 **C** 8

B -16 **D** 16

34. Solve: $x + 2.5 = 1.5$.

Skill 18

F -4 **H** 4

G -1 **J** 3

Section C: Rational Numbers and Exponents

SKILL 20: Evaluating Expressions with Exponents

To evaluate expressions with exponents, it is necessary to extend the order of operations rules to include exponents.

1. Do operations inside parentheses.

2. Evaluate terms with exponents.

3. Multiply and divide from left to right.

4. Finally, do all additions and subtractions from left to right.

To evaluate an expression that contains variables, first replace each variable in the expression with its value. Then use the order of operations.

Example 1

Evaluate $1 + 7(-3 + 5)^2$.

$1 + 7(-3 + 5)^2 = 1 + 7 \cdot (2)^2$ Do the operations within parentheses.

$= 1 + 7 \cdot (4)$ Evaluate 2^2.

$= 1 + 28$ Multiply.

$= 29$ Add.   So, $1 + 7(-3 + 5)^2 = 29$

Example 2

Evaluate $x^2 + 15$ for $x = 5$.

$x^2 + 15 = 5^2 + 15$ Replace the variable with its value.

$= 25 + 15$ Evaluate 5^2.

$= 40$ Add.   For $x = 5$, the value of $x^2 + 15$ is 40.

Guided Practice

1. Evaluate $1 + 2^3 \cdot (7 - 13)$.

$1 + 2^3 \cdot (7 - 13)$

$= 1 + 2^3 \cdot (\_\_\_\_)$

$= 1 + \_\_\_\_ \cdot (\_\_\_\_)$

$= 1 + (\_\_\_\_)$

$= \_\_\_\_$

$1 + 2^3 \cdot (7 - 13) = \_\_\_\_$

2. Evaluate $5x^2 + 1$ for $x = -2$.

$5x^2 + 1$

$= 5 \cdot (\_\_\_\_)^2 + 1$

$= 5 \cdot (\_\_\_\_) + 1$

$= \_\_\_\_ + 1$

$= \_\_\_\_$

For $x = -2$, the value of $5x^2 + 1$ is ____.

SKILL 20: Practice

Evaluate each expression.

1. $(4 + 6)^3 =$ _____

2. $(-8 + 5)^2 =$ _____

3. $4 + 6^3 =$ _____

4. $1 + 5^3 =$ _____

5. $40 + 3 \cdot 2^2 =$ _____

6. $16 - 7 \cdot 2^3 =$ _____

7. $(12 - 5)^3 =$ _____

8. $(16 - 7) \cdot 2^3 =$ _____

9. $(2 + 3)^2 - 7 =$ _____

10. $(16 - 7 \cdot 2)^3 =$ _____

11. $48 + (-2)^3 =$ _____

12. $(2^3 + 4^2) \div 4 =$ _____

13. $(1 + 6)^2 \cdot 3 =$ _____

14. $2^3 + 4^2 \div 4 =$ _____

15. $(3 + 3^2) \div 3 =$ _____

16. $2^5 - 1 =$ _____

Evaluate each expression. Use the given value for each variable.

17. $41 + m^2$ for $m = 3$ _____

18. $(17 - k)^3$ for $k = 12$ _____

19. $(x + 4)^2$ for $x = 8$ _____

20. $(5 + 2n)^5$ for $n = -2$ _____

Solve.

21. A company plans to assign a 5-digit ID number to each employee. The first digit will never be 0. The expression $9 \cdot 10^4$ represents the number of possible ID numbers. How many ID numbers are possible? _____

22. If you have two dice of different colors, there are $6^2 - 6$ ways to roll two different numbers. In how many ways can you roll two different numbers? _____

23. Evaluate $(1 + 3 \cdot 2)^2$.

Skill 20

A 13   **C** 49

B 37   **D** 56

24. What is the standard form for $(-2)^3$?

Skill 19

F −6   **H** 6

G −8   **J** 8

© Prentice-Hall, Inc.

SKILL 21: The Pythagorean Theorem

The **hypotenuse** of a right triangle is the side opposite the right angle and is the longest side. The other two sides are called **legs**. In the triangle at the right, sides *a* and *b* are the legs. Side *c* is the hypotenuse.

The **Pythagorean Theorem** states that the sum of the squares of the lengths of the legs of a right triangle is equal to the square of the length of the hypotenuse. This can be written algebraically as $a^2 + b^2 = c^2$.

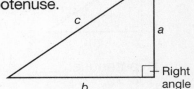

Example 1

> **Name the hypotenuse and legs of the right triangle.**
> Side *h* is opposite the right angle, so it is the hypotenuse.
> Sides *i* and *j* are the legs.

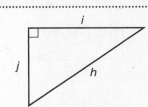

Example 2

> **Find the length of side *c*.**
>
> | | |
> |---|---|
> | Use the Pythagorean Theorem. | $a^2 + b^2 = c^2$ |
> | Substitute 9 for *a* and 12 for *b*. | $9^2 + 12^2 = c^2$ |
> | Square 9 and 12. | $81 + 144 = c^2$ |
> | Add. | $225 = c^2$ |
> | Find $\sqrt{225}$. | $15 = c$ |
>
> The length of the hypotenuse is 15 cm.

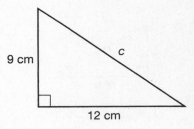

Guided Practice

1. Name the hypotenuse and legs of the right triangle.

    a. The side opposite the right angle is side ____.

       So, the hypotenuse is side ____.

    b. The legs of the right triangle are sides ____ and ____.

2. Find the missing length in the right triangle.

Use the Pythagorean Theorem. $a^2 + b^2 = c^2$

Substitute 4 for *b* and 5 for *c*. $a^2 +$ _____ = _____

Replace each squared number with its value. $a^2 + 16 = 25$

Undo the addition. Subtract ____ from both sides. $a^2 + 16 - \mathbf{16} = 25 - \mathbf{16}$

                                         $a^2 =$ ____

To find *a*, find the square root of 9. $\sqrt{9} =$ ____

The missing length is ____ in. $a =$ ____

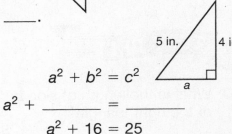

Name _____ Date _____ Class _____

SKILL 21: Practice

Name the hypotenuse and legs of each right triangle.

1.

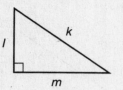

Hypotenuse: ____

Legs: ____ and ____

2.

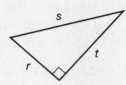

Hypotenuse: ____

Legs: ____ and ____

Find the missing length in each right triangle.

3.

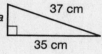

$a =$ _____

4.

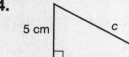

$c =$ _____

5.

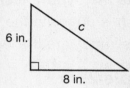

$c =$ _____

6.

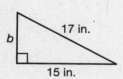

$b =$ _____

7.

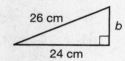

$b =$ _____

8.

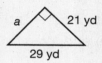

$a =$ _____

9. A courtyard that is 12 feet by 16 feet has a diagonal walkway. What is the length of the walkway? _____

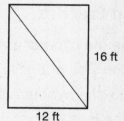

10. What is the length of side b of the right triangle?

Skill 21

A 1 cm   C 9 cm

B 7 cm   D 11 cm

11. Evaluate $4 + x^2$ for $x = 8$.

Skill 20

F 60   H 68

G 20   J 144

Section C: Rational Numbers and Exponents

Circle each correct answer.

1. Find $\frac{1}{4} + \left(-\frac{3}{4}\right)$ in simplest form.

Skill 17

    A $-\frac{1}{2}$ **C** 1

    B -1 **D** $\frac{1}{2}$

2. Evaluate $(5 - 3x)^2$ for $x = -5$.

Skill 20

    F -400 **H** 100

    G -100 **J** 400

3. What is $6 \cdot 6 \cdot 6 \cdot 6 \cdot 6$ in exponential form?

Skill 19

    A 5^6 **C** $5 \cdot 6$

    B 6^5 **D** $6 \cdot 5$

4. Find the missing length in the right triangle.

Skill 21

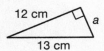

    F 1 cm   **H** 294 cm

    G 5 cm   **J** 25 cm

5. Which number is less than -8?

Skill 16

    A $-8\frac{1}{4}$ **C** $-6\frac{1}{2}$

    B $-7\frac{9}{10}$ **D** 7

6. Solve: $3x = -\frac{1}{2}$.

Skill 18

    F $-1\frac{1}{2}$ **H** $\frac{1}{6}$

    G $-\frac{1}{6}$ **J** $\frac{2}{3}$

7. What is 100^2 in standard form?

Skill 19

    A 200   **C** 10,000

    B 1,000   **D** 20,000

8. Find $-\frac{5}{6} + \frac{1}{6}$ in simplest form.

Skill 17

    F 1   **H** $-\frac{2}{3}$

    G $\frac{2}{3}$ **J** $-\frac{5}{12}$

9. Solve: $m - \frac{5}{6} = -2$.

Skill 18

    A $2\frac{5}{6}$ **C** $-1\frac{1}{6}$

    B $1\frac{1}{6}$ **D** $-2\frac{5}{6}$

10. Evaluate $1 + (1 - x)^3$ for $x = 2$.

Skill 20

    F -6 **H** 2

    G 0   **J** 8

11. The temperature fell 12.5°F over a 5-hour period. The temperature change was the same for each of these hours. What was the temperature change each hour?

Skill 17

    A $-2.5°F$ **C** 2.5°F

    B $-25°F$ **D** 60°F

12. Find $\sqrt{49}$.

Skill 19

    F 2,401   **H** 7

    G 98   **J** 9

Mixed Review for Section C

When does a rational number like to have a triangle as a friend?

To find out, complete each exercise. Write the letter for each answer on the blank above the answer at the bottom of the page.

I   **1.** -3.8 written as the ratio of two integers _____

I   **2.** Solution of $-3x = -18$ _____

L   **3.** Standard form for $(-1)^8$ _____

I   **4.** Value of $-\frac{1}{3} \cdot \left(-\frac{1}{2}\right)$ _____

T   **5.** Value of $-4 \div \frac{2}{3}$ _____

A   **6.** $(-3) \cdot (-3)$ in exponential form _____

T   **7.** Value of $1 + (-2 + 4)^5$ _____

E   **8.** Solution of $\frac{x}{9} = \frac{-1}{3}$ _____

N   **9.** Length of the hypotenuse of a right triangle whose legs have lengths 12 cm and 16 cm _____

G   **10.** Length of the hypotenuse of a right triangle whose legs have lengths 30 cm and 40 cm _____

R   **11.** Solution of $8x = -6$ _____

R   **12.** Value of $\left(-\frac{4}{5}\right)^2$ _____

S   **13.** Value of $\left(-\frac{1}{5}\right)^3$ _____

H   **14.** Value of $4\frac{1}{3} - 5\frac{1}{3}$ _____

G   **15.** Value of $(-4 + 9)^3 - 25$ _____

When the ___ ___ ___ ___ ___ ___ ___ ___
            33 $\frac{16}{25}$ 6 $(-3)^2$ 20 cm 50 cm 1 -3

___ ___ ___ ___ ___ ___ ___ .
$\frac{1}{6}$ $-\frac{1}{125}$ $-\frac{3}{4}$ $-\frac{19}{5}$ 100 -1 -6